1/10

I0603175

GROSS BODY SCIENCE

Itch & Ooze

GROSS STUFF ON YOUR SKIN

Written by Kristi Lew

Illustrated by Michael Slack

Millbrook Press • Minneapolis

To Dad — thanks for soothing and medicating countless blisters, mosquito bites, and sunburns over the years. I love you. -Kristi Lew

To Ethan, Ally, Nellie, Tristan, Dillon, Ryan, and Hannah
-Michael Slack

Text copyright © 2010 by Kristi Lew
Illustrations copyright © 2010 by Michael Slack

Millbrook Press
A division of Lerner Publishing Group, Inc.
241 First Avenue North
Minneapolis, MN 55401 U.S.A.

Website address: www.lernerbooks.com

Library of Congress Cataloging-in-Publication Data

Lew, Kristi.
    Itch & ooze : gross stuff on your skin / by Kristi Lew ; illustrations by Michael Slack.
        p.   cm. — (Gross body science)
    Includes bibliographical references and index.
    ISBN 978-0-8225-8963-1 (lib. bdg. : alk. paper)
    1. Skin—Diseases—Juvenile literature. 2. Skin—Juvenile literature. I. Slack, Michael H.,
    1969- ill. II. Title. III. Title: Itch and ooze.
    RL86.L49 2010
    616.5—dc22   2008045591

Manufactured in the United States of America
1 2 3 4 5 6 — BP — 15 14 13 12 11 10

CONTENTS

CHAPTER 1
STRETCHY, STICKY, OFTEN ICKY
The Skin You're In page 4

CHAPTER 2
WET, SMELLY, AND COOL
Your Sweat page 18

CHAPTER 3
BLISTERS, CUTS, AND PUS
Skin Under Repair page 24

CHAPTER 4
STINGS, RINGS, AND ROT
What's Eating You? page 32

Glossary 42
Selected Bibliography 43
Further Reading 45
Index 47

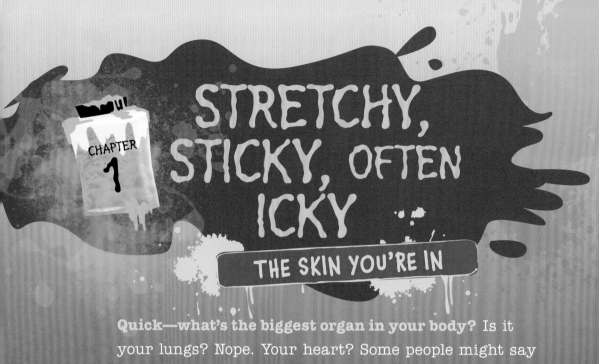

CHAPTER 1

STRETCHY, STICKY, OFTEN ICKY

THE SKIN YOU'RE IN

Quick—what's the biggest organ in your body? Is it your lungs? Nope. Your heart? Some people might say you have a big heart, but, no, that's not it. Your brain? You wish.

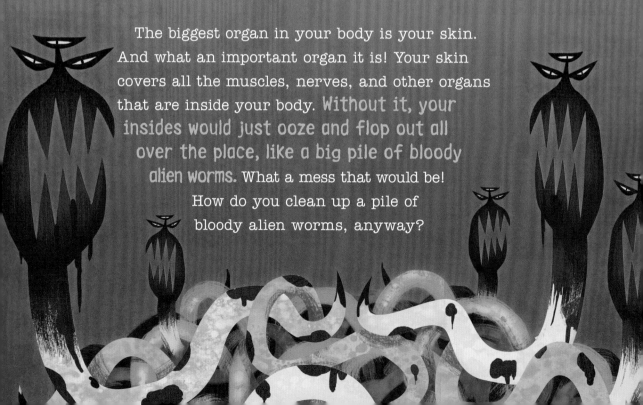

The biggest organ in your body is your skin. And what an important organ it is! Your skin covers all the muscles, nerves, and other organs that are inside your body. Without it, your insides would just ooze and flop out all over the place, like a big pile of bloody alien worms. What a mess that would be! How do you clean up a pile of bloody alien worms, anyway?

JUST HOW BIG *IS* SKIN?

Suppose you peeled the skin off an average adult. (I know, **YUCK!** But just imagine with me.) If you peeled off all that skin and stretched it out flat, it would be about 18 to 20 square feet (2 square meters). That would just about cover the hood (or roof) of a small car! And that bundle of skin would weigh about as much as a newborn baby (6 to 9 pounds, or 2.7 to 4 kilograms). Now, think about this: an adult's brain weighs about 3 pounds (1.4 kg). So an adult's skin weighs more than his or her brain! That doesn't surprise you? Well, you'd better not mention it to the really angry, bloody pulp of an adult you just skinned!

SKIN IS LAYERED... KIND OF LIKE LASAGNA

THE SKIN YOU'RE IN IS AWESOME. It helps your body stay at the right temperature. It gives you a sense of touch too. That's how you'd know if, for instance, a cockroach crawled up your leg. And of course, skin also protects the most gooey, goopy parts of you. It keeps your organs and tissues all together inside your body.

How does skin do all this? Well, it has a lot of parts. Skin is made up of three layers—the epidermis, the dermis, and the subcutaneous layers. Each layer has an important job to do.

The epidermis is the outermost layer of skin— the layer you can see and feel. Thanks to your epidermis, you can feel the wet, slimy kisses that your grandmother plants on your face. (Thanks, epidermis!)

The epidermis also has another important job. It creates new skin cells. Yep, day and night, your epidermis is hard at work making new skin cells (well, whenever it's not sensing big, sloppy grandma kisses). But why could you possibly need all those new skin cells? Didn't we already say your skin is your largest organ? **IT IS, BUT IT HAS A PROBLEM: DEATH.** Your skin cells die off faster than you can say, "Uh, thanks for the kiss, Grandma!"

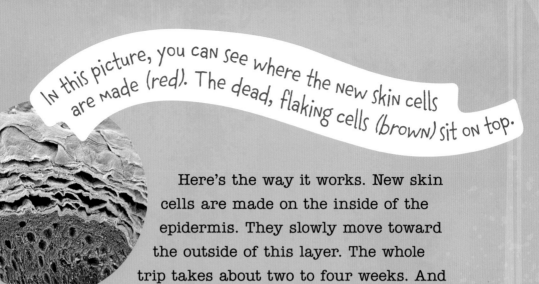

In this picture, you can see where the new skin cells are made (red). The dead, flaking cells (brown) sit on top.

Here's the way it works. New skin cells are made on the inside of the epidermis. They slowly move toward the outside of this layer. The whole trip takes about two to four weeks. And it's a pretty tough journey, because guess what? By the time they get there—they're dead! Yep, that's right. All the skin you see on the outside of your body is dead.

Luckily, these old, dead cells are tough and strong. They're just perfect for protecting the inside of your body. After a while, they flake off—just in time to be replaced by the new dead skin. Talk about the living dead! Who knew you were walking around with a graveyard covering your body? Hope it's not haunted!

GROSS FACT #1

Every minute of the day, you lose between thirty thousand and forty thousand dead skin cells. Every year, that adds up to almost 9 pounds (4 kg) of dead skin that you leave behind. There are dead skin cells smushed into your sofa, ground into your bedsheets, and stuck to your desk at school.

STRE-E-E-E-E-ETCH!

The layer under your epidermis is the dermis. The dermis is made up of strong, stretchy proteins called collagen and elastin. These help your skin to keep its shape. Without collagen and elastin, your skin wouldn't snap back to its original shape after it got stretched— say, after you bent your knees to pedal your bike. Instead, it would just hang there and flap like nice, baggy elephant knees.

Go ahead and stretch your skin. It will snap right back into place.

STRETCHIEST SKIN

Garry Turner (*right*) of Lincolnshire, England, has the stretchiest skin in the world. On October 29, 1999, Turner stretched the skin on his stomach to an amazing length of 6.3 inches (16 centimeters). Turner can do this because he has a rare condition that weakens the collagen in the skin. The weakened collagen allows the skin to stretch really far and then return to its normal shape.

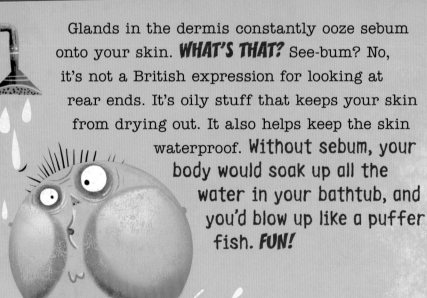

Glands in the dermis constantly ooze sebum onto your skin. **WHAT'S THAT?** See-bum? No, it's not a British expression for looking at rear ends. It's oily stuff that keeps your skin from drying out. It also helps keep the skin waterproof. **Without sebum, your body would soak up all the water in your bathtub, and you'd blow up like a puffer fish. FUN!**

A cross section of the skin shows the epidermis (top), dermis (middle), and subcutaneous (bottom) layers.

THE CUTE LAYER?

The third layer of skin lies below the dermis and is made up mostly of fat. Just about everyone agrees that a nice, thick layer of fat is cute. **So this bottom layer of skin is called the super-cutie layer.**

Wait, what? Oh, I mean the subcutaneous layer. **WHATEVER.**

All that cute fat helps keep your body warm. It also protects your muscles, bones, and organs. So, for instance, it doesn't hurt too badly when a fastball from the so-called best pitcher ever born smacks you in the thigh instead of sailing over home plate.

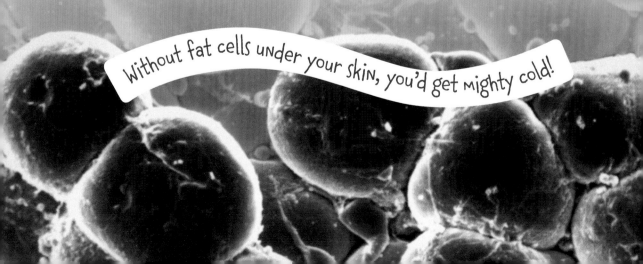

Without fat cells under your skin, you'd get mighty cold!

This fatty layer also helps anchor your skin to the structures underneath. If it didn't, your skin would just hang on your bones like an old, stretched-out bag. You'd always be pulling it up and adjusting it like a big, baggy skin costume.

Your hair is rooted in this fatty layer too. Hair sprouts from tiny tubes called follicles all over your body. Certain parts of your body, like your head, sprout more hair than others. But your fatty skin layer is chock-full of follicles even where you don't grow a lot of hair. Almost your whole body has hair, even if you can't see it. The only places you have no hair are the palms of your hands, the bottoms of your feet, and your lips.

Here's what a hair looks like growing under your skin.

11

GROSS FACT #2

You have more than one hundred thousand follicles just on your head. It's a real forest up there!

Remember that sebum oozing out of your skin? Well, it also oozes right onto your hair. This gives your hair some shine. It also makes it a little bit waterproof. But if you don't take a shower every couple of days, it just mats your hair down into a sticky, oily mess. **Talk about a bad hair day!** Of course, if you didn't shower and your bike chain needed oiling, you would be all set. Just rub a little hair grease on your bike chain, and you're good to go!

BELLY BUTTON LINT

Ever get bored? I mean, really bored. Sooo bored you think maybe you should check your belly button and see if anything fun is going on there? Hey, you never know, right?

AND, WELL, LOOK! What is that sticky ball of blue fluff in there? It's belly button lint. Thank goodness for skin! Without skin, there'd be no belly button lint! Actually, belly button lint is made up of dead skin cells, body hairs, and a whole lot of spare clothes fibers. Believe it or not, an Australian scientist actually took the time to ask more than forty-five thousand people about their belly button lint. Imagine that job. **"Excuse me, sir. How's your belly button lint doing? Mind if I take a peek?"**

So, what did he find? He found that more men than women have belly button lint. It seems to occur more often on more hairy people than on less hairy ones. Older people have more belly button lint than younger people. And you are more likely to have belly

What's hiding in YOUR belly button?

button lint if you have an "innie" rather than an "outie." So if you do not have enough belly button lint of your own to study, go find your granddad—or somebody else's granddad, for that matter. Just be polite about it.

Of course nobody's studied what belly button lint tastes like yet. Remember that the next time you're looking for a good science experiment. **YUMMY!**

TOE JAM

Speaking of goop that wedges into body cracks, what is that sticky, gooey stuff between your toes? A lot of people call it toe jam or toe cheese. Why is it a food name? And why not toe pizza? How about toe baloney?

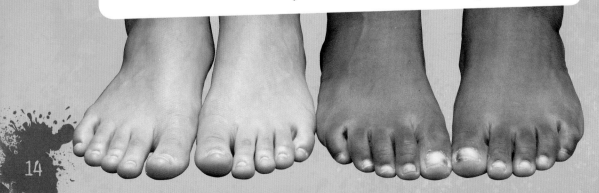

Scrub between your toes to avoid toe jam!

Whatever you want to call it, it's mainly made up of dead skin cells, sock lint, and sweat. And it turns out that toe jam *is* a kind of food. Tiny little bacteria cells just love to dine on this mixture. Have you ever smelled your toe jam? **NOT GOOD!** That's because bacteria make waste while they're eating. In other words, they poop. And the **bacteria poop** makes it stink. So, do you want some bread to go with that jam?

MOSQUITOES' FAVORITE CHEESE

You may not be the only one who enjoys the smell of that stuff between your toes. Scientists in the Netherlands did a study and found that mosquitoes are equally attracted to human feet and a smelly cheese called Limburger. Makes sense, say the scientists. Limburger smells a whole lot like toe cheese. Although that is interesting enough, the scientists are not planning to stop there. One day, they hope to copy the yummy smell of Limburger—or toe jam, whichever you prefer—and use it to make a better mosquito trap.

These mites are making a meal out of the oil around human hair.

MIGHTY SKIN MITES

Toe jam isn't the only part of you that attracts critters. Certain little bugs are just as happy dining on the sebum coming from your oil glands. These bugs are called **skin mites**, and they're so small you can't see them without a microscope. They can be found on just about any hairy part of your body. They love to feast on your head, of course. But they can also find a tasty meal inside your nose and ear canals or around your **eyelashes and eyebrows.**

Check out these bad boys. Up to twenty-five mites can live in a single follicle!

These flesh-colored mites live only on humans. Lucky us! And they can be found munching on the sebum of most people—about 97 percent of us—all over the world. It's an international buffet! The idea of having eight-legged little bugs chowing down all over your body might be gross, but they usually won't hurt you. If they reproduce too fast, you can get problems like acne and hair loss. But mostly, all your skin mites want to do is hang around with their friends and eat your sebum. Woo hoo! It's a party. There's plenty of food to go around.

CHAPTER 2

WET, SMELLY, AND COOL

YOUR SWEAT

Ever open the laundry hamper and feel like you're going to pass out from the smell? Deep breath . . . thunk. WHOA, WHAT'S THAT STENCH?

Well, it's probably coming from your sweaty soccer socks. Those suckers may not actually kill anybody, but they sure can knock you over! Why do they smell so bad? Lots of people think that it's because they're sweaty. And while sweat helps ripen the smell, that's not the whole story.

Remember that sebum that oozes out of your pores all day? Well, I hate to tell you this, but sebum isn't the only thing seeping out of your skin. You're also oozing sweat twenty-four hours a day, seven days a week. That's right, you're sweating all the time. **EEEW!**

A STICKY EXPERIMENT

Sweat and sebum both come out of tiny holes in your skin called pores. And when sweat and sebum mix, look out! They make a sticky kind of coating. Want to see this stickiness at work? First, use your fingers to turn a page in this book. Now, go wash your hands with soap and water. Dry them off really well. Ready? Okay: try to turn another page. It's not as easy, is it? That's because your sticky layer is gone. But if the idea of having a sticky layer on your skin grosses you out, you're out of luck. You can wash it off, but it will be back soon.

SO WHY DO WE SWEAT?

Sweat is produced by sweat glands. Makes sense, right? Sensible stuff, that sweat. And it's got a sensible job: sweat's job is to keep your body cool. After all, what's more refreshing than a nice spray of water, right? That's what sweat is—a little squirt of water to cool off a hot body.

GROSS FACT #3

People are born with 2 to 4 million sweat glands. That's a lot of sweat-making stuff!

Your brother may not be thrilled to find your sweaty soccer socks laying around. But sweating during a soccer game is not only normal—it's absolutely necessary.

The heat from a stove makes water turn into steam and evaporate. The heat from your body makes sweat evaporate.

Sweat doesn't make you cooler just by showing up. It has to evaporate, or change from a liquid to a gas. And it needs heat to do this. Think about a pot of water. What makes the liquid water turn into steam? Heat, right? The sweat sitting on your skin needs heat to turn from liquid to gas too. The heat comes from your body. As the heat escapes, you cool off. Without sweat, you'd overheat. (And without a way to wash those socks, your brother would hate you!)

Sweat glands are found all over your body. But some places have more than their fair share of sweat makers. For example, you have lots and lots of them in the palms of your hands, on the soles of your feet, and on your forehead. Believe it or not, those are some of the sweatiest spots on your body.

These white shapes are glands in the armpit. Sweat made in the brown cells oozes into the glands and out through the pores.

GROSS FACT #4

Your outer ear contains a special kind of sweat gland. Instead of oozing sweat, these glands ooze earwax.

WHY DOES SWEAT STINK?

Actually, sweat does not stink. Oh, you beg to differ? You want me to take a sniff of a basketball player's armpit after a game? Okay, okay. That would probably stink. But honestly, it's not sweat making that smell.

Certain kinds of bacteria live on certain body parts, like armpits. And the bacteria that lives on your body eats the sweat and other chemicals that come out of your sweat glands. When that happens, you'd better stand back. **THEY MAKE QUITE A STINK!** The stink comes from the bacteria breaking down the chemicals and producing waste. Yep, it's bacteria poop again. This sweaty stew not only stinks, it can have a yellowish color to it too. This is the reason the underarms of white T-shirts sometimes become stained yellow.

Here's a smell test for you: Take one bucket of pure sweat from a big, tough football player. Then take a couple drops of bacteria poop. Give each one a good sniff. I guarantee you, the bacteria poop will be stinkier every time.

CHAPTER 3

BLISTERS, CUTS, AND PUS

SKIN UNDER REPAIR

Have you ever done a face plant when skateboarding? Or slipped while running and scraped your hands and knees across the gravel? *OUCH!* That really hurts. Your skin probably didn't appreciate that you shredded it, but it didn't hold a grudge. It just got to work trying to repair the damage you had done.

CUTS AND SCRAPES? NO PROBLEM!

As soon as you tear your skin, your body sends special cells called platelets to the site of the wound. These cells are like the body's glue. They stick together and form a clot. The clot helps to stop more blood from pouring out. Eventually, this clot dries to a nice crusty scab. Scabs are like your body's natural

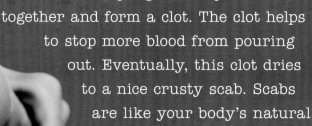

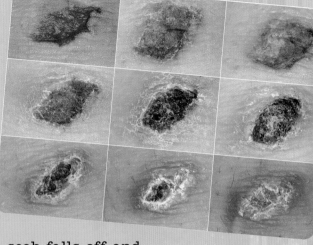

Here's what a scrape looks like as it heals.

bandages. Underneath the scab, your body is busy making new skin cells to fill in the gap you've made in your skin. When the new skin cells are ready, the scab falls off and—**TA-DAH!**—you're good as new.

LOST AND FOUND

The human self-repair kit is awesome. But did you know that some animals have the amazing ability to grow back lost body parts? If a bully crab pinches off another crab's claw, for example, the victim just grows another one. And crabs aren't the only talented ones. An earthworm can be cruising around your garden minding its own business when . . . whack! Some thoughtless gardener cuts him in half with a garden tool. How rude! But don't feel too sorry for Mr. Earthworm. These critters can grow back half of their body! Unfortunately, humans can't repair themselves nearly as well. So be careful of crabs and sharp garden tools!

A blister is kind of like a water balloon. Only, don't pop this one!

THE BLISTERING PAIN OF... BLISTERS

You don't have to skid across pavement to damage your skin. Something as simple as wearing the wrong-sized shoes can do it too. Shoes that don't fit right can cause blisters on your tender feet. When your skin gets really irritated, the outer layer can come apart from the inner layer. Ouch! Then the space in between the layers fills up with a watery liquid.

It sure is tempting to pop those suckers and spray your blister water at your little sister. But it's better for your body to leave a blister alone. That layer of skin covering an unpopped blister is like a shield against bacteria. If bacteria get into a nice raw blister, a painful infection is sure to follow.

When dealing with blisters, it's all about patience. If you can keep your hands from popping them for long enough, they'll heal themselves. Slowly, the outer layer becomes a little harder and forms tiny holes. The watery goop inside slowly escapes. Soon you're left with a small, hardened skin spot. Eventually, that softens and your skin is back in business.

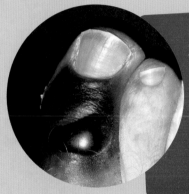

A BLISTER'S RED COUSIN

If your skin is pinched badly, blood vessels may break beneath the skin. Then you get a blister that is filled with blood instead of watery goop. Just like a regular blister, though, it's wise not to pop it.

PUS IS A MUST

So, what's the most disgusting substance you can imagine? Could it be that white stuff that oozes out of pimples or other wounds on your skin? **UGH! WHAT IS THAT GOO, ANYWAY?** It looks kind of like milk. But I wouldn't recommend pouring it over your cereal.

It's pus, and it sure is nasty to look at. Or to think about on your cereal (sorry about that!). But whether it's lurking inside an **OOZING, INFECTED BLISTER** or it's all over the bathroom mirror after your big brother pops a pimple, you need pus! It's a sign that your body is protecting you from bacterial infections.

Pus is mostly made up of white blood cells. Think of these as your body's soldiers in the war on infection. They surround and destroy bacteria that could make you sick. White blood cells are so tiny that they're invisible to the human eye. By the time enough of them have gathered under your skin so that you can see pus, many have already died in battle.

The next time you find yourself with a pus-filled pimple or other bump, remember this simple advice: Don't make a fuss. Don't cuss. Don't squeeze it on the bus. You need to keep that pus right where it is to fight infection.

Under a microscope, pus looks like this.

BAKING IN THE SUN

Most kids know they need protection from the sun. Or at least they know that grown-ups spend a lot of time slathering globs of sunblock all over them. **OW! MY EYES!**

But what are grown-ups so afraid of? What's the big deal about your skin getting a little pink? (Hint: there's a reason they call it sun*burn*.) Yep, a sunburn is actually burned skin. Charbroiled. Fried. Barbecued. **MMMM, PASS THE SAUCE, PLEASE!**

If you're lucky, getting sunburned just means you turn a little pink. Your skin might be a little tender, but you're usually back to your old self in about twenty-four hours.

If you're not so lucky, you can make yourself into a crispy little critter. Severe sunburns can mean anything from large, fluid-filled blisters to fever, nausea, chills, and dizziness. Sound bad? I forgot to mention that you also can go into shock and pass out. Really bad sunburns will most likely hurt like crazy.

Just when you think the torture is over, you start itching! Think that's bad? Just wait. Soon, long flakes of your skin will start to peel off. **GROSS!**

Of course, you could roll all that dead skin into a little ball and flick it like a booger at your buddy. Or, hey, maybe you could smooth it out and wallpaper your room. Hmm, maybe not.

"LEAVES OF THREE, LET IT BE"

So, you've recovered from that sunburn, have you? Better find somewhere else to hang out. Hey, how about that field covered in nice, soft, three-leafed plants? You and your friends can have great wrestling matches there.

Dude, bad choice! Ever heard the expression "leaves of three, let it be"? Well, if the field you're planning to roll around in has green, vinelike plants with three-pointed leaves, you might want to leave. **PRONTO!** That field is covered in poison ivy. And that is some bad news. Poison ivy has an oily, sticky chemical in its sap—excellent for sticking to skin.

About 50 to 70 percent of people are allergic to the chemical in poison ivy. But almost all people will become allergic if exposed to poison ivy enough times.

If you touch poison ivy, you might get a small red rash. Of course, your entire body may also turn as red as a lobster. Or you may grow huge golf ball–sized blisters. Everyone reacts just a little bit differently to poison ivy. Think you'd like to take a chance and see just how your body reacts? (I would not recommend this!)

CHAPTER 4

STINGS, RINGS, AND ROT

WHAT'S EATING YOU?

You might not mind a tiny little animal, like a skin mite, feeding on the excess oil in your hair. In fact it might be just great. But what about little critters who are helping themselves to your blood? Now that is rude! But it's exactly what lice, chiggers, and mosquitoes do.

A tiny mosquito can look pretty harmless . . . until you see one up close! Now where's that bug spray?

This familiar red welt means your blood has become some little insect's meal.

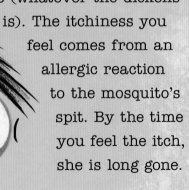

MOSQUITOES ARE NOT NEATO

You know that mosquito bites can make you really itchy. But did you know that only female mosquitoes bite? Yep, it's true. First, a female sticks her needlelike mouth under your skin. Then she squirts saliva, or spit, into you. Her spit has a chemical in it to keep your blood from clotting, or clumping up. This way, she can dine to her heart's content.

Of course, she leaves you with a small, red welt. Kind of like a zit. **THANKS, LADY!** And it itches like the dickens (whatever the dickens is). The itchiness you feel comes from an allergic reaction to the mosquito's spit. By the time you feel the itch, she is long gone.

33

These strands of hair are covered with lice and nits (louse eggs).

LICE ARE NOT NICE

All these party poopers like nothing better than to help themselves to your body buffet. Take head lice, for example. These terribly annoying creatures hang out in your hair and suck blood from your scalp, and you don't even feel it happening. And like mosquitoes, their spit contains a chemical that stops your blood from clotting. They bite through your skin, hawk a big fat loogie underneath, and suck away.

GROSS FACT #6

When there are more than one of those little creatures—and there usually are—they're called lice. But just one of them is a louse. That's where the word *lousy* comes from. As in: it's lousy having lice.

I'm having a LOUSY day!

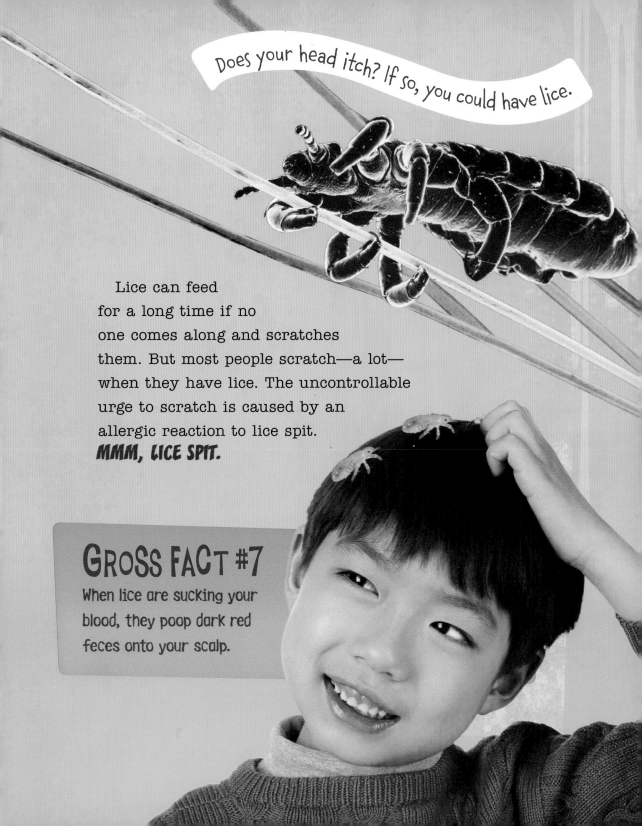

Does your head itch? If so, you could have lice.

Lice can feed for a long time if no one comes along and scratches them. But most people scratch—a lot—when they have lice. The uncontrollable urge to scratch is caused by an allergic reaction to lice spit. **MMM, LICE SPIT.**

GROSS FACT #7

When lice are sucking your blood, they poop dark red feces onto your scalp.

CHIGGERS

Chiggers (sometimes called red bugs) are too small to see with the naked eye. This leads many people to believe that they burrow under your skin and cause you to itch. But they don't. Like mosquitoes and lice, chiggers poke a hole into your skin to inject their spit.

However, these six-legged critters do not drink your blood. Oh no, that wouldn't be disgusting enough! Instead, their saliva contains a chemical that breaks down your skin cells into a mealy mush. **Their spit also has special chemicals that cause the tissue around the bite to harden into a tube. Once your skin cells have been liquefied, the chigger slurps up its tasty meal through its straw.** It's like a skin cell milk shake! **DELISH!**

Chigger bites

YOUR FUN FRIEND, GUS

Not everything that dines on your skin is an animal. A fun dude named Gus does too. What's that? His name isn't Gus? Well, what is it? Oh, fungus, not fun Gus. Whoops. When there's more than one kind of fungus, it's a fun guy. Uh, I mean fungi.

GUS

Anyway, some kinds of fungi live on the human body. Molds, mildew, yeast, and mushrooms are all types of fungi. But don't worry. That mushroom on your plate isn't going to leap up and clamp onto your face while you're trying to eat dinner. Instead, the type of fungus that will most likely get you is found in warm, damp places. Think of locker rooms and steam rooms. This is where the fungi that cause ringworm, athlete's foot, and jock itch like to hang out. Er—**YUCK!**

Here's a fungus that causes skin infections in animals and humans. It most commonly hangs out on the surface of the skin or nails.

Contrary to its name, ringworm is not caused by a worm. It's caused by a moldlike fungus. **YIKES**— suddenly a worm doesn't sound so gross, does it? Don't worry, getting ringworm on your scalp won't cause your head to look like a giant, moldy loaf of bread. But it can cause red, ring-shaped, itchy patches of skin and round areas of hair loss.

You can get ringworm on your nails too. Nail ringworm occurs more often on toenails than on fingernails. Nail ringworm can make nails thick and dull. Often the thickened, infected part of the nail turns yellow. Then it crumbles and flakes off from the rest of the nail. Not a pretty sight.

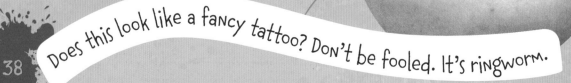

Does this look like a fancy tattoo? Don't be fooled. It's ringworm.

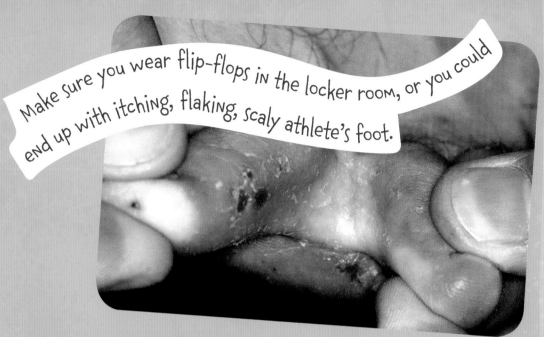

Make sure you wear flip-flops in the locker room, or you could end up with itching, flaking, scaly athlete's foot.

Another type of fungus likes to latch onto the skin between your toes. When this happens, you have athlete's foot. And if you are unlucky enough to get a fungal infection of the groin, you have jock itch. These conditions may sound funny now, but if you ever get them, you probably won't be laughing much! **SCRATCHING, YES. LAUGHING, NO.**

FLESH-EATING BACTERIA—YIKES!

If fungus isn't fun enough, how about bacteria? It rhymes with *cafeteria*, and that's exactly what some kinds of bacteria think your body is. One big cafeteria, where they can eat for free all day and all night. *Streptococcus* bacteria, for example, can cause lots of nasty problems.

On the mild side, this stuff can cause strep throat. But when *Streptococcus* gets mean, it gets really mean. A more serious condition caused by this type of bacteria is necrotizing fasciitis. Don't think that sounds very disgusting? Well, it's also known as flesh-eating disease. How does *that* sound? Yep, those bacteria can eat your flesh. **GROSS!**

THE MAN WITHOUT A FACE

Mark Tatum (*right*) of Owensboro, Kentucky, went through a lot. It all started when a flesh-eating fungus invaded his sinuses in 2000. The fungus quickly infected Tatum's eyes, nose, cheekbones, upper jaw, and teeth. Doctors were concerned that if the fungus spread to Tatum's brain, it would kill him. So they were forced to remove a large part of his face to save his life. Against all odds, Tatum lived another five years after his face was removed.

The bacteria Streptococcus pyogenes can lead to different kinds of infections, from strep throat to necrotizing fasciitis.

THE MIGHTY SKIN

As you can see, all kinds of things can make you itch and ooze. Your skin can be home to fungal infections, flesh-eating bacteria, and other kinds of disgusting things. Then, of course, there's sunburn, blisters, skin mites, and mosquito bites. But through it all, your skin holds up pretty well. If you treat your skin right, it'll return the favor by warding off most of those itchy, oozy problems.

GLOSSARY

acne: a skin condition that is the result of blocked oil glands in the skin

bacteria: tiny living things that live all over, including inside of you. Some bacteria are useful, and some are harmful.

dermis: the middle layer of skin

epidermis: the outermost layer of skin

feces: solid waste that leaves the body

fungus: a type of plant with no leaves, flowers, or roots. *Fungi* refers to more than one fungus.

glands: organs in the body that produce chemicals or allow substances to leave the body

hair follicle: a tube and opening in the skin that hair grows out of

necrotizing fasciitis: a condition also known as flesh-eating disease that's caused by *Streptococcus* bacteria

nits: lice eggs

pimple: a small, raised bump on the skin that is often reddish and may be filled with pus

pores: very small openings in the skin

pus: a thick, milky liquid made up of mostly dead white blood cells found at the site of an infection

sebum: natural oils that keep skin moist and protected

sinuses: eight hollow spaces above the eyes and on either side of the nose. The sinuses are connected to the nose.

Streptococcus: a kind of bacteria that can cause strep throat or more serious problems like flesh-eating disease

subcutaneous layer: a layer of fat and connective tissue that contains blood vessels and nerves; the deepest skin layer

SELECTED BIBLIOGRAPHY

Badash, Michelle. "Poison Ivy, Poison Oak, Poison Sumac." *NYU Medical Center.* 2008. http://www.med.nyu.edu/patientcare/library/article.html?ChunkIID=11616 (May 29, 2009).

Cohen, Elizabeth. "Getting a New Face After Rare Infection." *CNN Medical Unit.* February 8, 2002. http://archives.cnn.com/2002/HEALTH/02/03/prosthetic.face/index.html (May 29, 2009).

Kruszelnicki, Karl. "Bellybutton Lint—the Hole Story." *ABC Science.* N.d. http://www.abc.net.au/science/k2/

Lyon, William F. "Chiggers." *Ohio State University Extension*. N.d. http://ohioline.osu.edu/hyg-fact/2000/2100.html (May 29, 2009).

Penn State College of Medicine. "Fungal Infection." *Penn State Milton S. Hershey Medical Center*. October 31, 2006. http://www.hmc.psu.edu/healthinfo/f/fungalinfection.htm (May 29, 2009).

Rush, Aisha. "Demodex Folliculorum." *University of Michigan Museum of Zoology*. 2000. http://animaldiversity.ummz.umich.edu/site/accounts/information/Demodex_folliculorum.html (May 29, 2009).

UMMC. "Anatomy of the Skin." *University of Maryland Medical Center*. February 19, 2008. http://www.umm.edu/dermatology-info/anatomy.htm (May 29, 2009).

U.S. National Library of Medicine. "Sweating." *Medline Plus*. April 26, 2007. http://www.nlm.nih.gov/medlineplus/ency/article/003218.htm (May 29, 2009).

Weems, H. V., Jr., and T. R. Fasulo. "Human Lice." *University of Florida, Institute of Food and Agricultural Sciences*. June 2007. http://edis.ifas.ufl.edu/in261 (May 29, 2009).

FURTHER READING

BAM! Body and Mind
http://www.bam.gov/
Created by the Centers for Disease Control and
Prevention, BAM! Body and Mind answers questions
about health issues and helps kids make healthy
lifestyle choices.

Branzei, Sylvia. *Grossology and You*. Los Angeles: Price
Stern Sloan, 2002. Read all about blood, pus, guts,
warts, and other gross-out subjects.

Dolphin, Colleen. *Armpits to Zits: The Body From A to Z*.
Edina, MN: ABDO, 2008. Look up illustrated definitions
of body parts from A to Z. Fascinating facts provide
further information.

Hall, Margaret. *Skin Deep: Functions of Skin*. Chicago:
Raintree, 2006. Your skin is amazing! Read this book to
learn all about skin and how it works.

Infection, Detection, Protection
http://www.amnh.org/nationalcenter/infection/
Created by the American Museum of Natural History,
this website presents information on bacteria, viruses,
and fungi that can invade the human body and cause
disease.

KidsHealth
http://www.kidshealth.org/kid/
This site offers articles, movies, and games reviewed
by physicians and other health experts about medical,
emotional, and developmental issues that affect kids.

Masoff, Joy. *Oh, Yuck!: The Encyclopedia of Everything
Nasty*. New York: Workman Pub., 2000. Learn about
fifty disgusting things, including zits and body lint.

Parker, Steve. *Skin, Muscles, and Bones*. Milwaukee:
Gareth Stevens Pub., 2005. Read about the human body,
inside and out.

Szpirglas, Jeff, and Michael Cho. *Gross Universe: Your
Guide to All Disgusting Things Under the Sun*. Toronto:
Maple Tree Press, 2005. This is a fun book about all
sorts of gross things connected to the human body.

INDEX

allergic reactions: to lice spit, 35; to mosquito spit, 33; to poison ivy, 31
armpits, 21–23
athlete's foot, 39

bacteria, 15, 23, 26, 39–41
belly buttons, 12–14
bites, 33–36
blisters, 26–31
blood vessels, 27

chiggers, 36–37
cuts and scrapes, 24–25

dead skin, 6–8, 13, 15, 29, 30
dermis, 8–9

earwax, 22
epidermis, 6–7

follicles, 11, 12, 17
fungus, 37–39

hair, 11–12, 13, 16. *See also* lice

infection, 26, 28; fungal infection, 37–38
itching, 30, 31, 33, 35, 36, 41. *See also* allergic reactions

jock itch, 39

lice, 34–35

mosquitoes, 15, 32–33

necrotizing fasciitis, 40

oil glands, 9, 16
oozing, 12, 26–29, 41. *See also* pus

peeling skin, 30
pimples, 28
platelets, 24
poison ivy, 30–31
pores, 19, 21
pus, 27–28

ringworm, 38

scabs, 24–25
sebum, 9, 12, 16–17, 19
skin, 4–11, 41; layers, 6–11; size of, 4–5; stickiness of, 19; stretchiness of, 8–9
skin mites, 16–17
Streptococcus bacteria, 39–40
subcutaneous, 10–11
sunburn, 29–30
sweat, 18–23; smell of, 22–23
sweat glands, 19–23

toe jam, 14–15

About the Author

Kristi Lew is the author of more than two dozen science books for teachers and young people. She studied biochemistry and genetics in college and later worked in genetics laboratories and taught high school science. When she's not writing, she enjoys sailing with her husband. She writes, lives, and sails in Saint Petersburg, Florida.

About the Illustrator

Michael Slack's illustrations have appeared in books, magazines, and advertisements, and on TV. His paintings and drawings have been exhibited in the United States and Europe. Slack lives in the San Francisco Bay area.

Photo Acknowledgments

The images in this book are used with the permission of:© David Scharf/Peter Arnold, Inc., pp. 1, 3; © Susumu Nishinaga/Photo Researchers, Inc., p. 5 (top); © Soyka/Shutterstock Images, p. 5 (cockroach bottom left); © Lily Rosen-Zohar/ Shutterstock Images, p. 5 (cockroach bottom right); © Andrew Syred/Photo Researchers, Inc., p. 6; © Eye Of Science/Photo Researchers, Inc., p. 7; © Steve Gschmeissner/Photo Researchers, Inc., pp. 8 (top), 16 (top), 22; © Kaz Chiba/The Image Bank/Getty Images, p. 8 (bottom); © aberpix/Alamy, p. 9; © Dr. Don Fawcett/ Visuals Unlimited/Getty Images, p. 10 (top); Hossler Phd. /Custom Medical Stock Photo , p. 10 (bottom); © Dr. Gladden Willis/Visuals Unlimited/Getty Images, p. 11; © Pascal Preti/Photolibrary, p. 13; © iStockphoto.com/J. Paul Moore, p. 14 (bottom); © iStockphoto.com/andrew dean, p. 16 (bottom); © Andrew Syred/Photo Researchers, Inc., p. 17; © Eye of Science/Photo Researchers, Inc., p. 19; © iStockphoto.com/Nell Redmond, p. 21 (top); © Astrid & Hanns-Frieder Michler/Photo Researchers, Inc., p. 21 (bottom); © Miguel Sobreira/Alamy, p. 23; © iStockphoto.com/Constantin Cojocaru, p. 24; © Edward Kinsman/Photo Researchers, Inc., p. 25; © Catchlight Visual Services/Alamy, p. 26; © Dr P. Marazzi/Photo Researchers, Inc., p. 27; © Simko/Visuals Unlimited, Inc., p. 28; Istockphoto.com/Martti Salmela, p. 29; © iStockphoto.com/Tammy Bryngelson, p. 30; Custom Medical Stock Photo, p. 31 (left); © Joy Brown/Shutterstock Images, p. 31 (center) ; © Jack Schiffer/ Dreamstime.com, p. 31 (right); © Medical RF/Peter Arnold, Inc., p. 32; © Debe Yeske/ Visuals Unlimited, Inc., p. 33; © C. James Webb/Phototake, Inc., p. 34; Reflexstock/ © Image Source Royalty-free, p. 35 (boy scratching head); © Tim Flach/Stone/Getty Images, p. 35 (top); © Darlyne A. Murawski/National Geographic/Getty Images, p. 35 (lice on head); © Dr. Dennis Kunkel/Visuals Unlimited, Inc., pp. 36 (top), 37; © ISM/ PhototakeUSA, pp. 36 (bottom), 38 (bottom), 39; © Gary Gaugler/The Medical File/ Peter Arnold, Inc., p. 38 (top); AP Photo/Messanger-Inquirer, Bryan Leazenby, p. 40; © Fred Hossler/Visuals Unlimited, Inc., p. 41 (top); © Kenneth E. Greer/Visuals Unlimited, Inc. p. 41 (bottom).

Front cover: © Andy Roberts/Stone/Getty Images (feet), © iStockphoto.com/ Arlindo71 (head louse), © iStockphoto.com/Douglas Allen (mosquito), © iStockphoto. com/ Lev Ezhov (wood ticks), © iStockphoto.com/Matjaz Boncina (dry cracked skin), © iStockphoto.com/Jose Manuel Gelpi Diaz (sunburned boy), © iStockphoto.com/ Jallfree (lotion tube), © Dr. Dennis Kunkel/Visuals Unlimited, Inc. (background